Robbery FILE
The Museum Heist

by Amanda Howard

Consultant: Dr. John P. Cassella
Principal Lecturer in Forensic Science
Staffordshire University, England

BEARPORT

New York, New York

Credits

Cover, © Chris Pancewicz/Alamy and © Amsterdam, Van Gogh Museum (Vincent van Gogh Foundation); Title Page, © Amsterdam, Van Gogh Museum (Vincent van Gogh Foundation); 4, © Dattatreya/Alamy; 5T, © Rolf Adlercreutz/Alamy; 5B, © Shutterstock; 6L, © Shutterstock; 6R, © Shutterstock; 7, © Bridgeman Art Library, London/SuperStock; 8, © INTERFOTO Pressebildagentur/Alamy; 9T, © ImageState/Alamy; 9B, © Shutterstock; 10, © Amsterdam, Van Gogh Museum (Vincent van Gogh Foundation); 11T, © Amsterdam, Van Gogh Museum (Vincent van Gogh Foundation); 11B, © Shutterstock; 12, © Shutterstock; 13T, © Shutterstock; 13B, © Shutterstock; 14T, © Mikael Karlsson/Arrestingimages; 14B, © Shout/Rex Features; 15, © Jeremy Sutton Hibbert/Arrestingimages; 16T, © Shutterstock; 16B, © Tek Image/Science Photo Library; 17T, © ADC/Rex Features; 17B, © Susumu Nishinaga/Science Photo Library; 18, © Ticktock Media Archive; 19L, © ADC/Rex Features; 19R, © Thierry Prat/Sygma/Corbis; 20, © Shutterstock; 21T, © Niilo Tippler/istockphoto; 21B, © Frances Twitty/istockphoto; 22, © Arthur Turner/Alamy; 23B, © Rex features; 24, © David Cheskin/PA Wire/PA Photos; 25, © Ton Koene/Picture Contact/Alamy; 28L, © Shutterstock; 28R, © Ticktock Media Archive; 29, © Anatomical Travelogue/Science Photo Library; 30L, © Shutterstock; 30R, © Tek Image/Science Photo Library.

Every effort has been made by ticktock Entertainment Ltd. to trace copyright holders. We apologize in advance for any omissions. We would be pleased to insert the appropriate acknowledgments in any subsequent edition of this publication.

Publisher: Kenn Goin
Editorial Director: Adam Siegel
Project Editor: Dinah Dunn
Creative Director: Spencer Brinker
Original Design: ticktock Entertainment Ltd.

Library of Congress Cataloging-in-Publication Data

Howard, Amanda, 1973–
 Robbery file : the museum heist / by Amanda Howard.
    p. cm. — (Crime solvers)
 Includes bibliographical references and index.
 ISBN-13: 978-1-59716-550-1 (lib. bdg.)
 ISBN-10: 1-59716-550-6 (lib. bdg.)

1. Robbery investigation—Netherlands—Amsterdam—Case studies—Juvenile literature. 2. Art thefts—Netherlands—Amsterdam—Case studies—Juvenile literature. 3. Van Gogh Museum, Amsterdam. I. Title.

HV8079.R62H69 2008
364.15'52092—dc22

2007020583

Contents

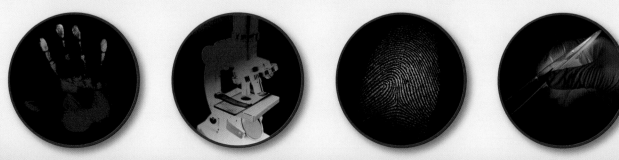

Before the Robbery

In 2002, two men visited the Van Gogh Museum in Amsterdam. Vincent van Gogh is a famous 19th-century Dutch artist. The museum is home to more than 100 of his paintings and letters. There are also paintings and sculptures from other artists. Many of them are worth millions of dollars.

Visitors at the museum admire a self-portrait of Vincent van Gogh.

To the museum's staff, the two men looked like any of the one million people who visit every year. However, these visitors had not come to admire the beautiful art. They were planning to steal two of van Gogh's paintings, worth $3 million each.

The Van Gogh Museum in Amsterdam

FACT FILE

Security Systems

Museums that display valuable works of art use many different kinds of security systems.

- Paintings or sculptures are often fitted with a wire that runs from the item to an alarm. The alarm is set off if the item is moved.

- Other security systems include **motion sensors**. These will sound an alarm when they sense that an object is being moved.

- Alarms can also go off when windows and doors are opened or broken. The windows and doors of the Van Gogh Museum were fitted with these types of alarms.

A motion sensor

A Simple Plan

In the days before the robbery, some staff members noticed a sledgehammer on the museum's roof. Others also saw a ladder leaning up against one of the walls.

At the time, some construction work was being done at the museum. Perhaps these tools had been left behind. No one thought to question why they were there.

A ladder was set up outside the museum on the night before the robbery.

A sledgehammer is larger and more powerful than a normal hammer.

The ladder and the sledgehammer were not being used for construction, however. They were part of a simple but clever plan to steal two van Gogh paintings. The thieves had put them there. On the morning of the **heist**, the men were able to walk up to the museum without looking **suspicious**. They didn't need to carry any tools for the break-in. They were already in place.

FACT FILE

Art Theft

- Art is often stolen for money. Sometimes art thieves ask for a **ransom** to return the art. Sometimes they sell the art to criminal art collectors.

- Less than 20 percent of stolen art is found.

- Many museums and galleries have high-tech security systems. Professional art thieves can outsmart these systems with careful planning.

- A famous painting by Edvard Munch called *The Scream* was stolen by thieves in 1994. The thieves left a note saying, "Thanks for the poor security."

The Scream, by Norwegian artist Edvard Munch

A Plan in Motion

The break-in at the museum took place in the early morning of December 7, 2002. As museum staff arrived for work at 7 A.M., the overnight **security systems** were shut down. Only a few alarms were left on.

The two thieves climbed up their ladder, which was leaning against a back wall of the museum. The building is next to a large park. That morning, it was filled with people jogging and walking their dogs. No one in the park noticed the men, however.

The Van Gogh Museum is next to a large park.

The robbers moved quietly to one of the skylights on the roof. One man held a cloth over the glass, while the other smashed the skylight with the sledgehammer. The cloth was meant to muffle the sound of the breaking glass. However, several people in the park heard the crash. They even stopped to watch the men enter the museum through the roof.

The thieves smashed the glass of the skylight.

FACT FILE

Automatic Police Alert Systems

- Museums are a common target for thieves. When an alarm goes off, not only does it make a loud noise, it also sends an **automatic** message to the local police.

- At the Van Gogh Museum, there were alarms attached to all the points of entry, such as doors and windows. As soon as the skylight was smashed, alarms were set off in both the museum and the police station.

Security guards are trained to capture and hold criminals until the police arrive. They cannot make arrests.

The Heist

When the museum's skylight was broken, the sound of security alarms began screeching throughout the building. The thieves dropped through the broken skylight. They moved quickly to the main gallery, where most of the valuable paintings were hanging.

The two men knew exactly what they wanted. As security guards and staff ran towards the main gallery, the thieves went straight to two paintings—*View of the Sea at Scheveningen* and *Congregation Leaving the Reformed Church in Nuenen*.

View of the Sea at Scheveningen was one of the two paintings taken by the thieves.

Police cars raced towards the museum with their sirens wailing. Each man grabbed a painting. The thieves knew that they had less than two minutes to escape before the police arrived.

Congregation Leaving the Reformed Church in Nuenen

FACT FILE

The Paintings

- Vincent van Gogh painted *View of the Sea at Scheveningen* in August 1882. Scheveningen is a small seaside town in Holland. Van Gogh stood on the beach to paint it. Particles of sand blew up and were mixed into the thick paint.

- *Congregation Leaving the Reformed Church in Nuenen* was painted at two different times. Van Gogh did the original painting during January and February 1884. In 1885, he changed the winter scene to an autumn scene by adding red and yellow leaves to the trees. He also added more people.

The beach in Scheveningen

The Escape

With the paintings in their hands, the two thieves made their way to a side window. They smashed the glass and tied a rope around a pole. They then climbed out of the window and down to the ground.

An **eyewitness** outside the museum watched in amazement as the men ran to their getaway car and drove away with the two paintings. The robbery had taken less than seven minutes. Closed-circuit cameras had captured the whole crime on film.

The police arrived quickly, hoping to arrest the thieves. Yet they were too late. The men were gone, leaving behind two empty spaces on the walls of the museum.

The thieves climbed down a rope to make their escape.

The police were automatically alerted when the museum's alarms went off.

FACT FILE

Closed-Circuit Television

- Closed-circuit television is a common security system. Cameras film an area. Security guards watch the images from these cameras on television screens.

- When security guards see a crime being committed, they sound an alarm.

- Some cameras record without stopping, like a movie. Other cameras take photographs every few seconds.

A closed-circuit camera

The Investigation

After the robbery, museum staff moved other paintings around to cover the gaps in the main gallery. They then opened the museum to visitors.

Crime-scene investigators began searching for clues to identify the art thieves. They reviewed the film from the closed-circuit camera. They also searched the museum for physical **evidence**.

Crime-scene investigators search for evidence.

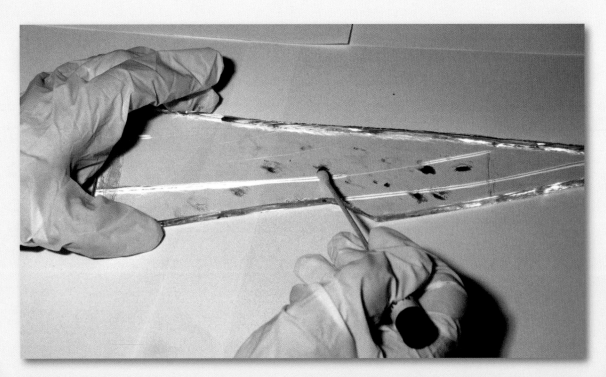

Shards of glass from the skylight and window were examined by forensic scientists.

The first piece of evidence they found was the ladder. It was examined for **fingerprints** and shoe prints.

Both men had left their shoe prints. Copies were taken of the prints so they could be matched to any possible **suspects** in the case. The glass from the smashed skylight and the window the men had escaped through were taken away for **forensic** testing.

One police officer dusts a window for fingerprints while another takes photographs.

The DNA Evidence

The two thieves wore caps to hide their faces from the cameras. However, during their escape, one man lost his cap while climbing out of the window. The other man lost his cap on the street as he ran to the getaway car.

One of the thieves wore a dark-blue Nike cap.

Investigators found the caps when they searched the museum. They were taken to the police forensic laboratory. Hairs from the thieves were found inside the caps and tested for DNA.

A forensic scientist places a single hair into a sample container.

The DNA was compared to samples of other known criminals. A match for some of the hair was found. Now police had the name of a possible suspect—and their first break in the case.

A scientist uses a computer database to compare two DNA samples.

FACT FILE

One Tiny Hair

A single hair can provide enough DNA evidence to identify a criminal.

- When criminals are arrested, the police take a DNA sample from them. Information about their DNA is kept in a national **database**.

- The police can check DNA samples from other crimes against this database.

- The Dutch police checked the DNA from the hairs in the thieves' caps against their database. It matched the DNA sample of a known art thief!

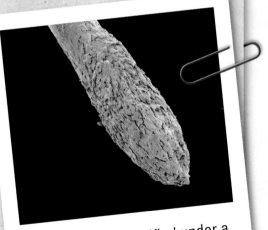

A single hair, magnified under a microscope

To Catch a Thief

On December 12, 2003, newspapers reported that Spanish police had arrested one of the van Gogh art thieves. Dutchman Octave Durham was arrested in Marbella, a popular holiday resort in Spain. He had been on the run for more than a year.

The DNA evidence from one of the hats had led police to Durham. He was a known criminal, and a suspect in many other art thefts.

Marbella, Spain

Knowing that Durham was their main suspect, the Dutch police tapped his phone to find him. By secretly listening to his cell phone calls, they were able to track him down in Spain. He was arrested and flown back to the Netherlands to face charges.

A police officer listens to a phone tap.

An Arrest in Amsterdam

After the arrest of Octave Durham in Spain, Dutch police arrested another suspect in Amsterdam. It was Henk Bieslijn, a 31-year-old Dutchman.

Bieslijn had been identified on the tapped phone conversations with Octave Durham. Police also matched Henk Bieslijn to the hair DNA evidence that he had left at the museum.

Bieslijn was still in Amsterdam when police captured him.

The police had now caught both thieves. However, Durham and Bieslijn claimed they were innocent. They also refused to say where the paintings were hidden.

It is against the law in the Netherlands to release images of art thieves.

FACT FILE

International Police Cooperation

- Criminals sometimes leave the country in which their crime was committed. When this happens, police forces from different countries must work together to capture them.

- The Dutch police couldn't legally arrest Octave Durham after he fled Amsterdam.

- The Dutch police shared what they knew about Durham with the Spanish police. They then arrested Durham.

- Durham was sent back to the Netherlands, where he was charged with the theft of the paintings.

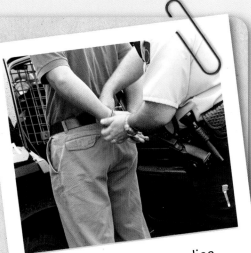

Dutch and Spanish police planned the arrest together.

Thieves for Hire

Why did Henk Bieslijn and Octave Durham steal the van Gogh paintings? No one knows for sure. However, experts on art theft believe many paintings are stolen at the request of art collectors. The market for stolen art around the world is valued at $12 billion every year.

The paintings were probably removed from their frames to make it easier to hide and transport them.

The police watched Bieslijn and Durham closely before they arrested them. After the theft, the two men began spending a lot of money on travel and expensive items like designer watches. This was evidence that the men had sold the paintings to a collector for a lot of money.

FACT FILE

The Reward

- The Van Gogh Museum has offered $130,000 for the safe return of the paintings. So far, nobody has claimed the reward.

- International police departments, such as the United States' **FBI** and Europe's **Interpol**, are still searching. The two van Gogh paintings are on their list of the ten biggest art heists around the world. Most of the paintings on the list are worth millions of dollars.

- Dutch law says that thieves can keep stolen paintings if they aren't recovered within 30 years.

The FBI and other organizations are working together to try to find the paintings.

The Trial

Octave Durham and Henk Bieslijn stood trial for the art theft in July 2004. Lawyers presented DNA evidence from the hair found in the caps at the crime scene. The phone-tap recordings of the two men discussing the robbery were played for the **jury**. Closed-circuit television images of the men leaving the museum were also shown. The evidence against Durham and Bieslijn was very convincing.

Closed-circuit television recordings of the robbery were shown in court.

On July 27, 2004, Octave Durham and Henk Bieslijn were found guilty of stealing the van Gogh paintings. Octave Durham was **sentenced** to four-and-a-half years in jail. Henk Bieslijn received a four-year sentence. Durham's sentence was longer because he had taken part in other art robberies. Each man was ordered to pay a fine of $455,000 to the Van Gogh Museum.

FACT FILE

Eyewitness Evidence

Witnesses can play an important role at a criminal trial. Several eyewitnesses gave evidence at the Van Gogh Museum art-theft trial.

- Witnesses told how they heard the thieves break the skylight and saw them enter the building.

- One witness described how he saw Durham and Bieslijn leave the building, jump into a getaway car, and drive away.

A witness tells police what she saw.

Case Closed

December 7, 2002

Two thieves break into the Van Gogh Museum in Amsterdam, Holland, and steal two paintings by Vincent van Gogh.

December 2002 to November 2003

Police search the museum for clues. The thieves are caught on closed-circuit television. They left several items behind: a cloth, a ladder, a sledgehammer, and two caps. There were hairs in the caps, which gave the police DNA evidence.

December 2003

Octave Durham is arrested in Marbella, Spain. The DNA in one of the caps matches his profile.

Henk Bieslijn is arrested by the Dutch police in Amsterdam. They had heard him discussing the robbery with Octave Durham on his phone.

July 2004

The trial of Henk Bieslijn and Octave Durham begins. Both men are found guilty of the robbery. Durham is sentenced to four-and-a-half years in prison. Bieslijn is given a shorter sentence—four years.

Today

The paintings are still missing.

Crime Solving Up Close

Crime-Scene Investigation

A crime scene is the place where evidence of a crime is found. There may be several crime scenes in one investigation. In the van Gogh robbery, the main crime scene was the museum where the robbery was committed. The following often happens at a crime scene.

- Police mark off the crime scene with caution tape. This stops any evidence from being damaged or taken from the scene.

- The crime-scene investigation team carefully searches for any evidence that may help solve the crime. This may take several days.

- The team wears special plastic clothing and masks. It is important that they don't spoil the evidence with their own fingerprints, hair, or fibers from their clothes.

- The police examine surfaces like walls for blood, fingerprints, and footprints.

- All evidence found at the crime scene is placed in evidence bags and labeled. The evidence bags are tightly sealed to prevent anyone from damaging the contents.

- The evidence is then transported to a forensic laboratory, where it is examined by scientists.

POLICE LINE DO NOT CROSS

Crime scenes are marked off with caution tape.

A crime-scene investigator seals an evidence bag.

Hair Evidence

In the Van Gogh Museum case, the investigators found hairs at the crime scene. These hairs provided clues that helped to prove the guilt of Octave Durham and Henk Bieslijn.

- Hair is one of the most useful types of forensic evidence that can be left at a crime scene. It can be found on glass or in clothing or debris.

- Forensic scientists may study hairs under a comparison microscope. This is a special microscope with two eyepieces. Scientists use this to compare hairs from a suspect with hairs from the crime scene. If the hairs match, this provides evidence that the suspect could have been present at the crime scene.

- Scientists look at the thickness, color, and shape of the hair.

- It is sometimes possible to tell the sex, race, and age of criminals from their hair.

- Hairs can also be analyzed for DNA.

Human hair shown under a microscope

Crime Solving Up Close

DNA Matching

A sample of DNA from the criminal's hair was enough to lead police to the art thieves.

- DNA is a unique chemical code people carry in cells of their bodies. People get their DNA from their parents.

- Scientists only need a tiny amount of DNA, which can be found in a drop of blood or a single eyelash, to create a DNA profile.

- When criminals are convicted, the inside of their mouths are wiped with a cotton swab. This gives the police a sample of their DNA.

- When the police have a DNA profile from a crime scene, they compare it to the national computer database. This contains the DNA profiles of millions of known criminals.

A computer model of a small section of DNA

A DNA profile can provide powerful evidence.

Glossary

automatic (aw-tuh-MAT-ik) a function preset to be performed without anyone doing it

crime scene (KRIME SEEN) an area where an illegal act has taken place

database (DAY-tuh-bayss) information stored in a computer

evidence (EV-uh-duhnss) objects or information that can be used to prove whether something is true

eyewitness (*eye*-WIT-niss) a person who sees something and describes the scene

FBI (EF BEE EYE) abbreviation for Federal Bureau of Investigation; an organization that looks into violations of federal law for the United States Department of Justice

fingerprints (FING-gur-*prints*) the impressions made by the pattern of curved ridges on the tips of one's fingers

forensic (fuh-REN-sik) using science and technology to help solve crimes

heist (HYEST) a robbery

Interpol (IN-ter-pohl) an international organization that coordinates the police activities of more than 100 nations

jury (JU-ree) a group of people that listens to facts at a trial and makes a decision about who is to blame

motion sensors (MOH-shuhn SEN-surz) instruments that detect movement

ransom (RAN-suhm) money that is demanded for the return or release of a person or object being held

security systems (si-KYOOR-i-tee SISS-tuhmz) a group of alarms that help keep something safe

sentenced (SEN-tuhnsst) a court's decision about the amount of time a guilty person must serve in jail as punishment for a crime

suspects (SUHSS-pekts) people who are thought to have committed a crime

suspicious (suh-SPISH-uhss) acting in a way that causes question or doubt

trial (TRYE-uhl) an examination of evidence in a court of law to decide if a charge is true

Index

Read More

Lane, Brian, and Laura Buller. *Crime & Detection.* New York: Dorling Kindersley (2005).

Owen, David. *Police Lab: How Forensic Science Tracks Down and Convicts Criminals.* Canada: Firefly Books (2002).

Oxlade, Chris. *Detective Tool Kit: Investigate Everyday Mysteries with Forensic Science.* Philadelphia, PA: Running Press Book Publishers (2005).

Learn More Online

To learn more about crime solving and the van Gogh case, visit
www.bearportpublishing.com/CrimeSolvers

About the Author

Amanda Howard writes extensively about true crime, including the encyclopedia *River of Blood: Serial Killers and Their Victims*. She is currently studying for her Bachelor of Social Science in Criminology, Criminal Law, and Psychology. She lives near Sydney, Australia, with her family.